Build-a-Skill Instant Books

Word Families—Long Vowels

Written by
Amy Lubben and Rozanne Lanczak Williams

Editors: Vicky Shiotsu and Stacey Faulkner
Illustrators: Jenny Campbell and Darcy Tom
Cover Illustrator: Rick Grayson
Designer: The Development Source
Art Director: Moonhee Pak
Project Director: Betsy Morris

Table of Contents

Introduction

About the Build-a-Skill Instant Books Series

The *Build-a-Skill Instant Books* series features a variety of reproducible instant books that focus on important reading and math skills covered in the primary classroom. Each instant book is easy to make. Once children become familiar with the basic formats that appear throughout the series, they will be able to make new books on their own with little help. Children will love the unique, manipulative quality of the books and will want to read them over and over again as they gain mastery of basic learning skills!

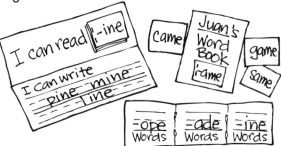

About Build-a-Skill Instant Books: Word Families—Long Vowels

This book features 27 common long vowel word families to use with four fun and easy-to-make instant book formats.

Special Feature This book's special feature allows you to reproduce the word family cards included at the back and use them with any of the instant book formats!

Children will develop fine motor skills and practice following directions as they cut, fold, and staple the pages together to make flip books, mini books, and more. As children read and reread their instant books, they will strengthen their decoding skills and increase their sight word vocabulary.

Refer to the Table of Contents to help with lesson planning. Choose instant book activities that fit with the curriculum goals in your regular or ELL classroom. Use the instant books to practice skills or to introduce new ones. Directions for making the instant books appear on pages 3 and 4. These should be copied and sent along with the book patterns when assigning a bookmaking activity as homework.

Making and Using the Instant Books

All of the instant books in this resource require only two or three pieces of paper. Copy the pages on white copy paper or card stock, or use colored paper to jazz up and vary the formats. Children will love personalizing their instant books by coloring them, adding construction paper covers, or decorating them with collage materials such as wiggly eyes, ribbon, and stickers. Customize the instant books by adding extra pages, or by creating your own word cards using the reproducibles on pages 31 and 32.

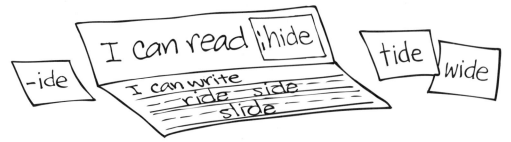

Children can make instant books as an enrichment activity when their regular classwork is done, as a learning center activity during guided reading time, or as a homework assignment. They can place completed instant books in their classroom book boxes and then read and reread the books independently or with a reading buddy. After children have had many opportunities to read their books in school, send the books home for extra skill-building practice. Encourage children to store the books in a special box that they have labeled "I Can Read Box."

Directions for Making the Instant Books
There are four basic formats for the instant books in this guide. The directions appear below for quick and easy reference. The directions are written *to* the child, in case you would like to send the bookmaking activities home as homework. Just copy the directions and attach them to the instant book pages.

Flip Books, page 5

1. Cut out the two flip books, word cards,
   and lined word cards.

2. Staple the word cards to the "I can read" flip book.

3. Staple the lined word cards to the "I can write"
   flip book.

4. "Flip up" each card to practice reading and writing your words.

Mini Flip Book (makes 2), page 6

1. Cut out the mini flip book and word cards.

2. Staple the word cards to the mini flip book.

3. Practice reading your words.

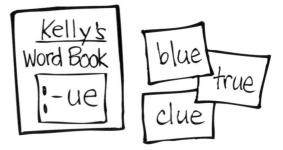

Read-and-Write Book, page 7

1. Cut out the read-and-write book.

2. Glue the book to a piece of construction paper the same size.

3. Cut out the word cards. Staple the cards to the top strip.

4. Fold the book in half and decorate the cover.

5. Practice reading and writing your words.

Word Wallet, page 8

1. Write a word family on each section of the wallet.

2. Cut out the word wallet. Fold it in half along the solid middle line.

3. Staple where shown. Tape the outer edges.

4. Fold the wallet closed.

5. Cut out the word cards. Sort them into the correct pockets.

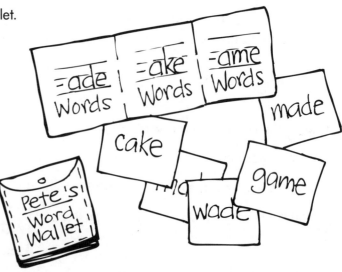

Build a Skill Instant Books • Word Families—Long Vowels © 2015 Creative Teaching Press

I can read

I can write

Staple word cards here.

Staple word cards here.

I can read ¦jade

made

wade

Mini Flip Book

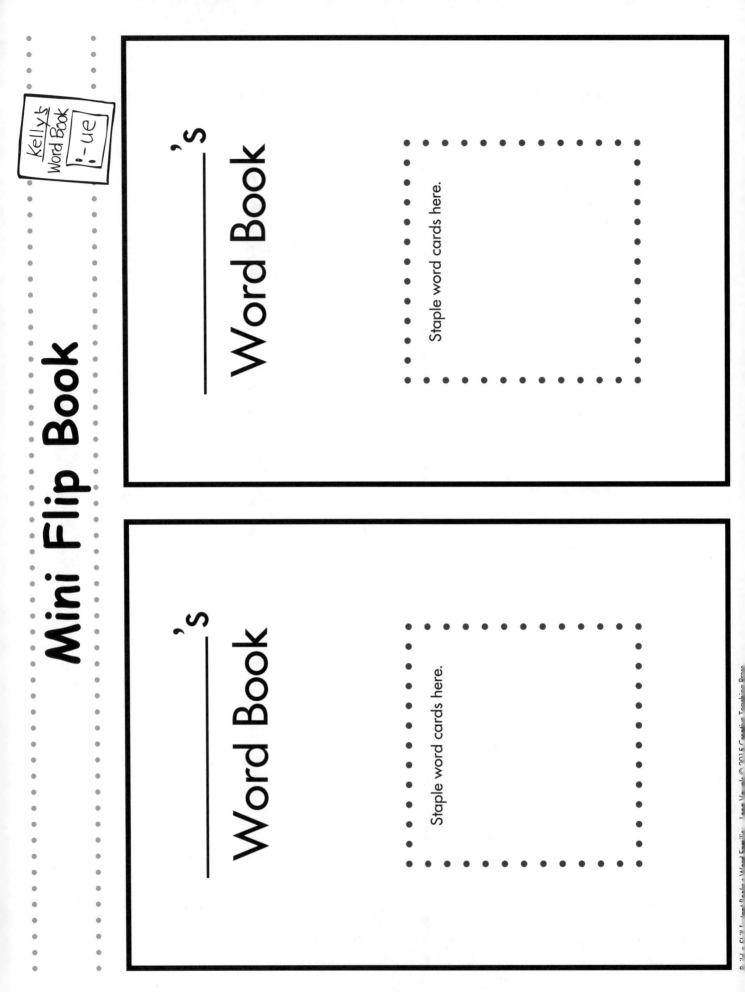

Kelly's
Word Book
i-ue

_____'s
Word Book

Staple word cards here.

_____'s
Word Book

Staple word cards here.

Read-and-Write Book

I can read

Staple word cards here.

I can write

I can read

I can write

Word Wallet

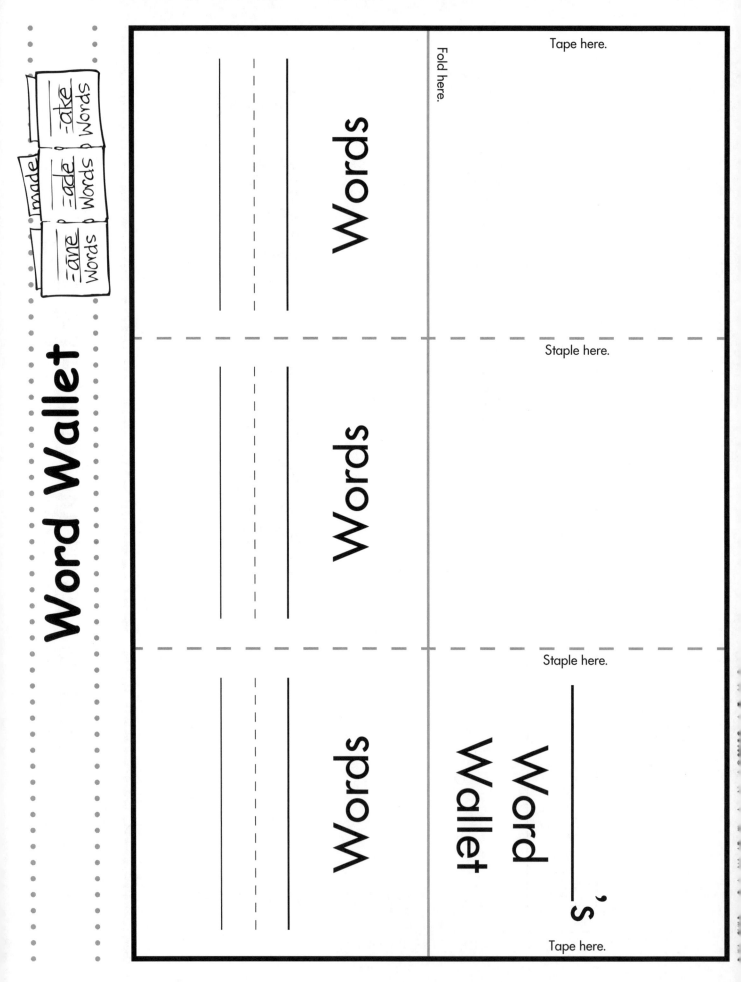

-ake Words

-ade Words

made

-ane Words

Words

Words

Words

Words

Words

Words

Tape here.

Fold here.

Staple here.

Staple here.

Tape here.

Word Wallet

_____ 's

-ade	blade	fade
grade	jade	made
shade	spade	wade

-ake	bake	cake
lake	make	rake
snake	take	wake

-ale Word Family

-ale	bale	gale
male	pale	sale
scale	tale	whale

-ame	came	fame
frame	game	flame
name	same	tame

Word Family

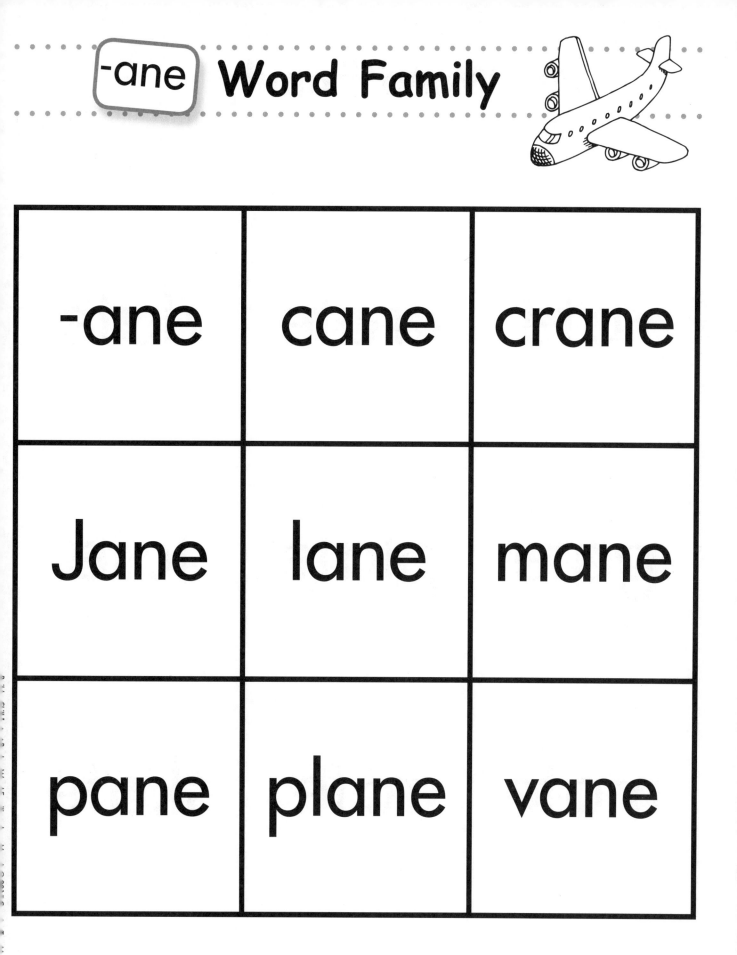

-ane	cane	crane
Jane	lane	mane
pane	plane	vane

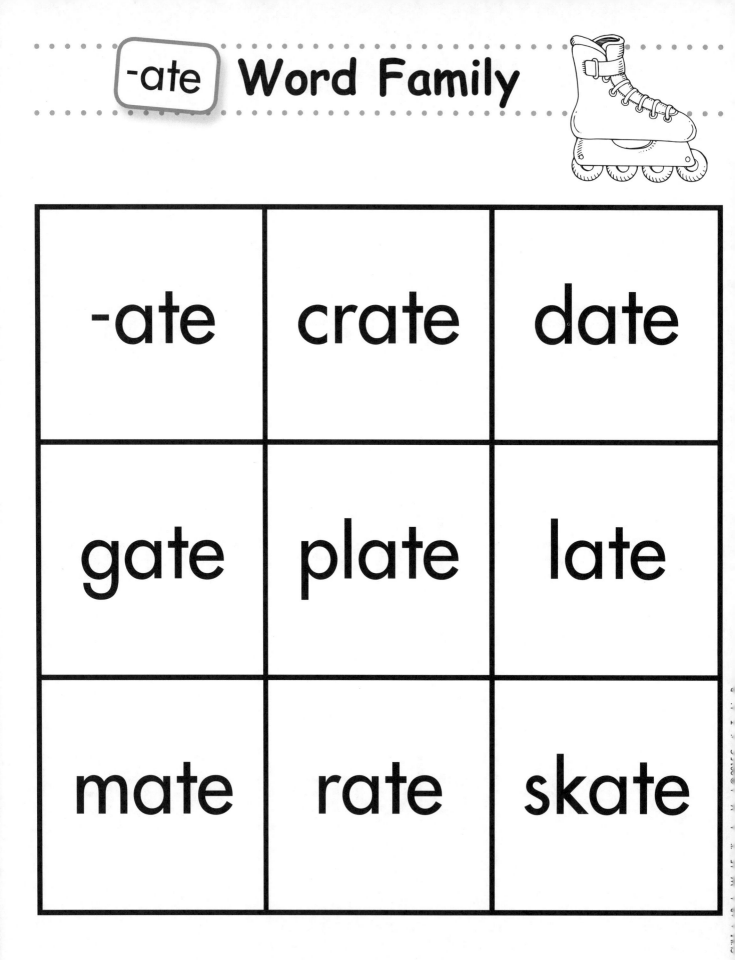

-ate	crate	date
gate	plate	late
mate	rate	skate

-ave	brave	cave
gave	grave	save
shave	pave	wave

-eat Word Family

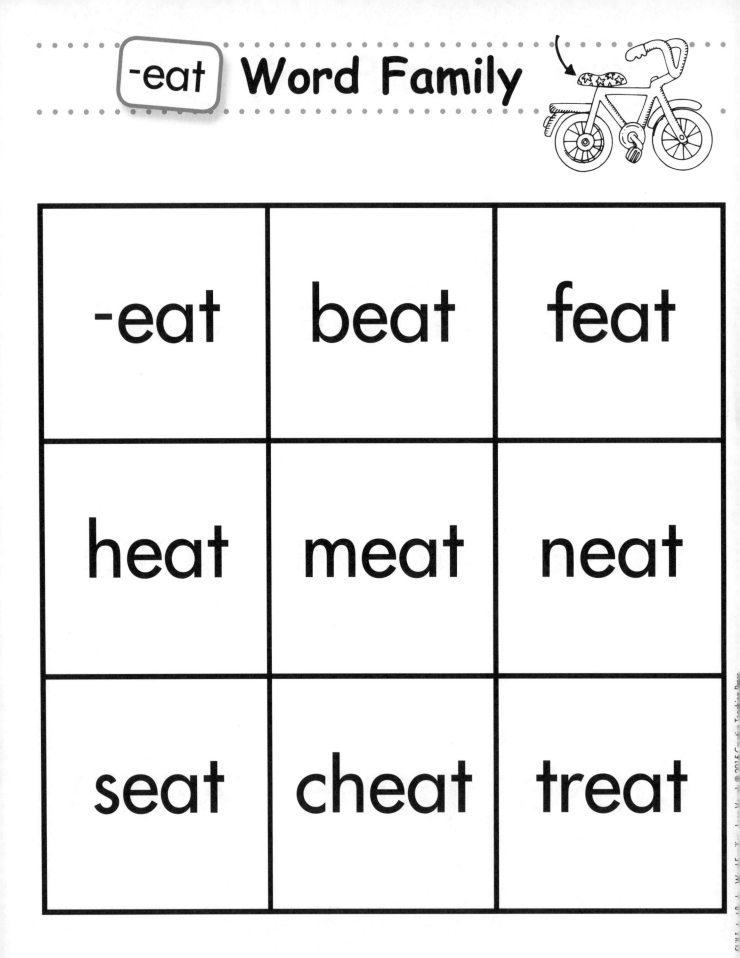

-eat	beat	feat
heat	meat	neat
seat	cheat	treat

-eed Word Family

-eed	feed	need
seed	weed	bleed
speed	deed	greed

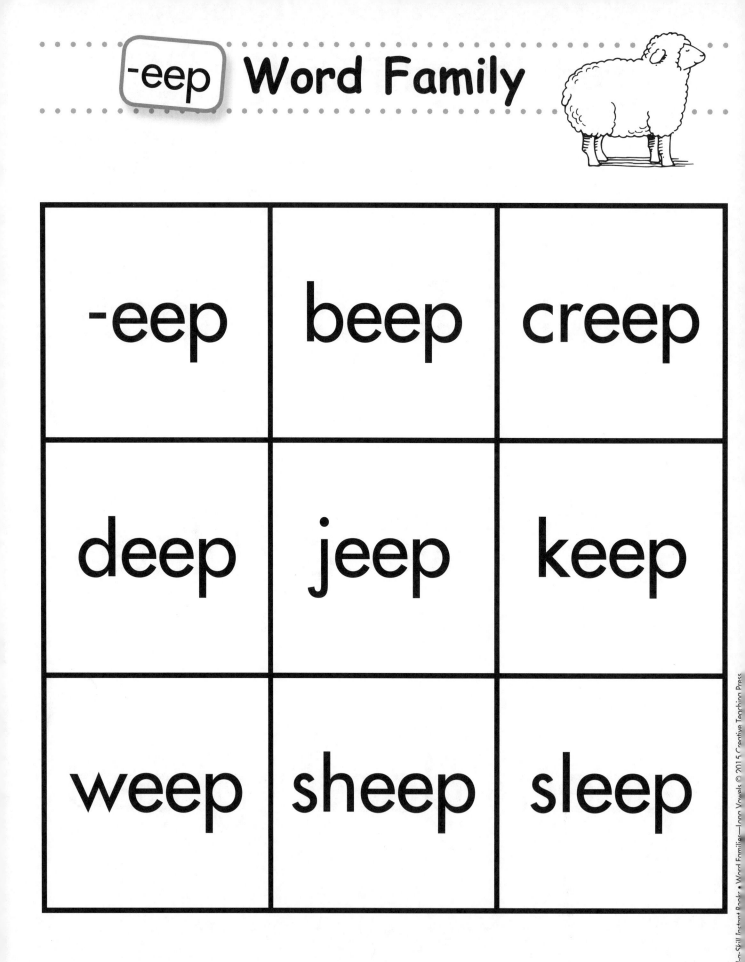

-eep	beep	creep
deep	jeep	keep
weep	sheep	sleep

Build-a-Skill Instant Books • Word Families—Long Vowels © 2015 Creative Teaching Press

-eet	beet	feet
meet	fleet	sheet
sleet	street	sweet

-ice Word Family

-ice	dice	ice
mice	nice	rice
price	slice	twice

Build-a-Skill Instant Books • Word Families—Long Vowels © 2015 Creative Teaching Press

-ide	bride	hide
ride	side	tide
wide	pride	slide

bike	hike	like
Mike	trike	file
mile	pile	while

-ime	chime	crime
dime	lime	mime
time	prime	slime

-ind	blind	find
hind	kind	mind
rind	wind	grind

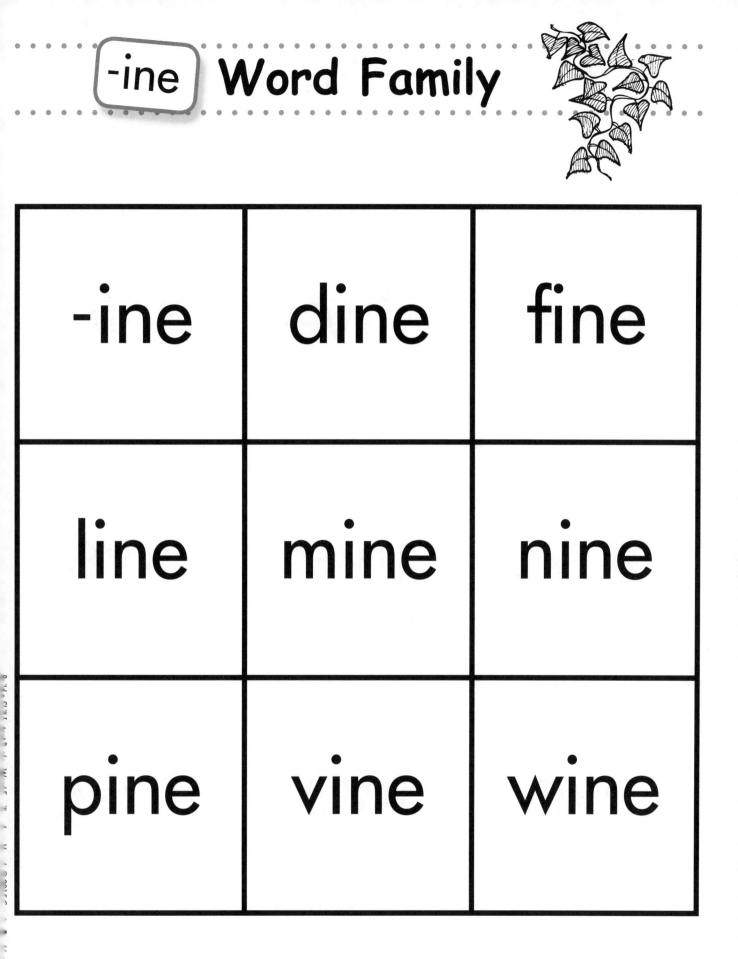

-ine	dine	fine
line	mine	nine
pine	vine	wine

-ive	alive	dive
drive	five	hive
jive	live	strive

Word Families

joke	poke	woke
smoke	yoke	hose
nose	rose	close

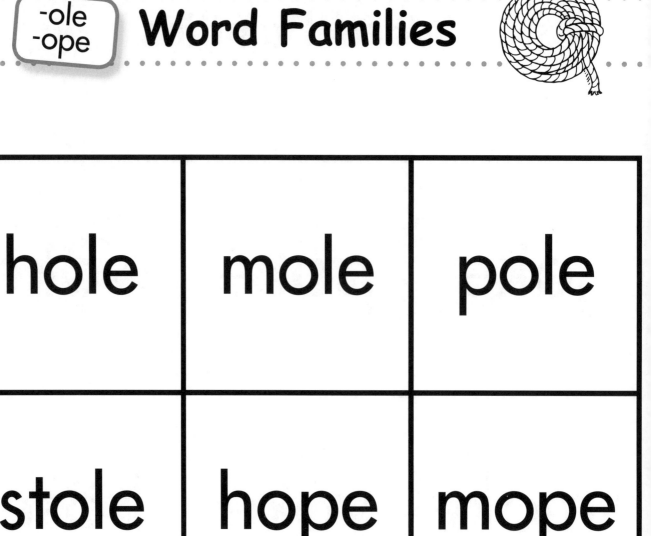

hole	mole	pole
stole	hope	mope
rope	scope	slope

-one	bone	cone
lone	phone	stone
throne	tone	zone

Word Families

cube	tube	blue
clue	due	true
cute	flute	mute

Word Cards

Word Cards